Limitless Questions

The Ultimate Guide to
Authentic Connection with
Friends, Family and Dates
Through Deep Question
and Answer

Andrew Noske, PhD &
Ann Swanson, MS

VERSION: 1.0.3 (updated 2022-07-21)

ISBN-13: 9781234567890 (kindle)
ISBN-13: 9798544614913 (paperback)

We want to dedicate this book to our friends in Hawaii. Hawaii immediately captured our hearts, and our friends in the fire dancing and spiritual community were pivotal in us meeting and coming up with the idea of our own deck of authentic related questions, plus this companion book. In particular, we want to thank our close friends: Taylor McClure and Fran Viererbl, who tried many of these questions on dates, and the wonderful spiritual duo Victoria Chin and Courtney Arakaki, who inspired us more than they know.

Hawaii quickly captures your heart, but it's as much about the people here as it is the spectacular scenery and beach culture.

QuickStart to Play!

There are infinite ways to use this book.
We suggest:

(1) Read it at home to highlight and memorize the best questions so you look like a badass.
(2) Keep it in your pocket to take on a date or to a meal with friends and play the game.

To play the game:

1. Choose someone to answer first, and someone to ask.
2. Have the asker flip through the book until they see a section that looks interesting, or use the table of contents and pick together.
3. Tell the answer how many questions are in the section and ask the answer to choose a question number. Keep in mind that the lower numbers in each section are usually pretty easy while higher numbers may be more challenging.
4. Ask them the question, and listen actively. If there's multiple people, you should always look at the answerer, and don't interrupt them. If two people, then once the

answer has finished, the answer is allowed to ask the same question back.

5. Switch people and repeat the process.

Remember that you can skip any question, just like in real life, but the challenge is to ride your edge. The game is done whenever you feel it is done. You really never know what questions are challenging to someone, but the questions most likely to trigger people are marked with a warning icon ($\triangle$), and if the question asker is not comfortable asking the question they may ask for another number.

If you don't have the book with you, we also have an online game which randomly selects questions. Head to:

www.limitlessquestions.com

Introduction

This book contains over 600 questions to help
deeply connect with someone beyond the typical
and often boring interactions you get from a
colleague ("*oh yeah George seems pleasant*") to
the unforgettable conversations you'd hope to
share when meeting a charismatic force of nature
("*oh wow, George is f**king amazing, you should
meet him*"). We also want you to understand that
this book is not just a list of questions to randomly
or mechanically flip through. This book will teach
you the principles of what makes an incredible
question-based conversation.

This book should be small enough to fit in your
pocket, because we want you to carry it with you
and play the game whereby you take turns and
randomly flip the pages and ask questions. That
said, you probably also want to read it at home
and we encourage you to take out a pen to mark
your absolute favorite questions. If you memorize
just two amazing questions you may suddenly
become that interesting girl at work, or the guy
that always gets second dates.

A great interaction goes beyond the words of a
question, and into the way in which you ask the
question, the way you actively listen, and your
ability to know what questions work in what
moments. The best people who talk and listen let

it flow naturally, and they understand that you can't start a conversation with "*tell me about your dead parents Batman*". In a way, using this book as a portable game, can feel safe, because you can always blame chance for an awkward question, such as asking someone about their mom's name just after they explained that they are orphaned.

In real life, in moments when you don't have this book, we want you to understand that getting to know someone better – whether your goal is a deeper friendship, flirty romance or an uplifting unforgettable interaction with a stranger – you need to learn how to escalate your level of vulnerability with someone. Just after the table of contents is a section with some principles that will help make these questions work well for you, and also help you expand on what's written so that you can come up with your own unique questions and follow up questions.

We also have a card deck and online game available at **www.limitlessquestions.com**, but only the book itself has practical advice on how to expand these questions into everyday life.

Preface

To understand this book, you'll want to understand its genesis and the motivations we both had.

From Andrew:

As a scientist and engineer, you maybe wouldn't peg me as someone who enjoys asking deep questions and breaking rules. If there's a taboo question you're not supposed to ask on a first date, I guarantee I've asked it. At immersive events like Burning Man (yes I'm one of those people) I love to ask people of all ages and backgrounds my "burning man question": can you describe each of their most significant romantic partners, with a single word each, in chronological order. I often ask the same question on a first date, in a more interactive way, and that single question can take up the entire night. Often one question is all it takes to deeply connect to someone. Just one amazing question and courage to be vulnerable.

The questions in this book are are great material to connect with your friends, family, workmates, a romantic interest or yourself. Few people these days seem to go beyond standard uninspired questions, like *"what do you do for work"*. Even fewer people know how to ask a good mix of playful questions and deep questions. If you can master that ratio and build up your repertoire of great questions, pretty quickly you can stand out as the person who is caring and brave enough to ask about the things that really matter. And when you genuinely listen to the answer, you create memorable connections.

At the end of 2020, as the initial pandemic panic was subsiding, I moved to Hawaii and found myself sitting on the beach with a group of lovely people and playing an "authentic relating game" called hot seat. In this game, each person had a ten minute turn to sit on the "hot seat" and everyone else raises their hands to ask personal questions. Several people came up after the game and complimented my questions. I wasn't afraid to dive in deep fast. That's not to say that I don't start with enjoyable playful questions, such as *"what is your superpower"*, but what excites me even more is when someone shares how they have grief or overcome difficult challenges in life and grown character through adversity. That is real to me.

I decided to document my questions in my wiki article and, as fate would have it, around that time I met the incredible Ann Swanson.

I appreciate so many things about Ann. She's become one of my closest friends. She is playful, intelligent, kind and driven. Ann is the kind of friend who gets you presents and leaves them under your pillow, like a ninja, for you to discover and smile the next day. Better yet, Ann shares two of three of my greatest passions: dancing, writing and deep cultivating connections. Ann is a driven entrepreneur and yoga goddess who has published a highly successful book called SCIENCE OF YOGA which has sold over 300,000 copies worldwide. I'm terrible at yoga, but what I love about Ann as my favorite dance partner and close friend is how we compliment each other.

Ann had the idea that we could make a card game with some of our questions, and for each question I've added into our big database of questions, she carefully looked at it and explained how I could ask it with greater sensitivity. I'm really excited we are making Limitless Questions together. Limitless questions includes this pocket sized book, an interactive website to generate random questions (**www.limitlessquestions.com**) and a deck of cards. The card deck includes only the very best conscious questions, whereas this book... contains almost everything! I hope you get great pleasure from this book, as we have got pleasure from testing these questions on friends.

From Ann:

As a yoga therapist I empower people to heal themselves by making yoga and mind-body practices non-intimidating and practical. I am constantly amazed by people's profound transformational experiences. Yoga truly works, but freeing your body is only one part of the equation. You also need to free the mind!

I've been a science nerd for as long as I can remember. I speak and teach on the key research supporting yoga and meditation, but I also am deeply interested in human connection. Not long after meeting Andrew, we found ourselves sitting with a group of friends after salsa and recreating a game called hot seat. Some of the questions we asked were so juicy and deep, I got immediately excited about developing more and more questions.

A small group of us started sending our best questions for dates to each other, and soon we realized we had acquired quite a brilliant wealth of knowledge and experience between us. This book represents a wonderful array of questions from the funny and bizarre to the deep and spiritual. Not every question suits every person and I really want to remind people to skip any question they feel uncomfortable with.

Chances are you are not a trained therapist, so when someone does go into a deep or dark place, it's really not your place to offer life advice. Leave that to licensed experts. All of us, however, can help just by listening with love and offering our emotional support. Reminding people that life will always present challenges, but it's up to us to learn, to grow and to get excited!

I know I've had limitless fun with these questions already. Many laughs, many tears, and many deep hugs. With the help of this book Andrew and I are hoping you can take your personal interactions beyond the shallow and forgettable and start making the most amazing deep friendships. Friendships that have the potential to last a lifetime.

Be limitless everyone!

Table of Contents

Guidelines to Connect Deeply

Here are 10 principles we want to cover in becoming amazing at asking questions, answering questions, and connecting deeply.

1. **Become an Active Listener (focus on them)**
2. **Learn How to Escalate Vulnerability**
3. **Pay Attention to Triggers**
4. **Be Vulnerable**
5. **Take on a Positive Growth Mindset**
6. **Balance The Heart Stuff With Playfulness**
7. **Be Daring and Guess (when appropriate)**
8. **Know When to Take A Break**
9. **Finish with Your Heart**
10. **Be Limitless**

1. Become an Active Listener (focus on them)

The last time you met a truly amazing listener you were probably memorized and never quite figured out why. Active listening is a skill few people have. If we had to guess, we would estimate that less than 1% of people are any good at it. Most people who ask a question don't make eye contact, let alone listen deeply. Instead we tend to "**listen-think**". Instead of really hearing and feeling into the other person's story we are constantly thinking about how we will respond and making ourselves the focus.

Their voice is saying *"I really wish my dad would quit smoking..."* but the self-obsessed voice in our head is simultaneously nagging at us with "*oh this reminds me of my own story about my mom not exercising, maybe I can interrupt at the end of the next sentence, or maybe it's rude, I will wait just a little longer*".

Every try to follow two conversations at once? It's exhausting. And you will fail every time.

According to scientists, multitasking is a myth, so let's try that again.

"I really wish my dad would quit smoking...".

Charismatic listeners lean into your words to encourage you to dig deeper. They don't interrupt you with their own agenda, they listen until the end of the story and then leave a pause after you speak. The pause is when they carefully craft a reply. The pause is what sets them apart.

"Oh that sucks Stacy. It sounds like you want to remind your dad that you love him and that you have friends that have died from lung cancer. You have a deep fear of losing him."

So let's recap:

1. Practice warm eye contact.
2. Pay attention by adopting open body language and leaning into their words.
3. Drop all judgment.
4. Calm your inner voice.
5. Make the conversation about them.
6. Leave a pause, and think of your reply after they finish.
7. The best reply is often to empathetically reflect or clarify what they have said.

When you are the asker of the question, this is how you should listen. In rare cases, if the answer starts to ramble, you can jokingly remind them they are off topic and they should appreciate the gentle reminder. And if you decide you want to be an active listener in all life, remember to balance it out with humor and banter. Don't turn these warm questions into an interrogation. Interrogators look almost angry and trained to stare someone down

Enjoy the book ?!

Please help support me as an amature author by **leaving a review** on Amazon via this QR code.   ☺

(bonus: order a copy for a verified review)

Here you'll also see my other titles:

Ice Cream ⊖ Sex

♥ Andrew

through intense cold silence until they break. You are not trying to break someone with these questions, you are playfully encouraging them to open up. Vulnerability is something you achieve with love, encouragement and a warm smile. Your body language should be soft, and you are allowed to laugh and smile. In times of trouble, people often don't want advice as much as a pair of empathetic ears, and an embracing heart.

2. Learn How to Escalate Vulnerability

Vulnerability with someone one is something you typically earn over time. For some people it is rarely earned, because they rarely go beyond surface level dialog such as gossip and shopping. With your new found active listening, you might be shocked how quickly you can share vulnerable conversations, but it does require you to pay attention to the escalation. Most people are comfortable with answering standard questions like *"where are you from"*, but until you build rapport, you wouldn't start a conversation with a stranger at "*how's your relationship with you father right now*". Each time you flip a page, you might want to quickly ask yourself *"is it too soon to go this deep"*. Or you just ask them if they are ready to go deep.

If you are playing "Limitless Questions" as a

game, you already have context and mindset of vulnerability, and that helps tremendously. If it's a conversation with a new friend without this book by your side, that's when you have to develop the skills to read the room and work out how and when you should escalate from a playful conversation to a deeper one. Ideally your interaction can be both of these things.

3. Pay Attention to Triggers

Old friends are amazing because you've probably built rapport over time and can ask them almost anything. But even with close friends, you should pay attention to what might really trigger them. This book encourages people to "ride their edge", but for someone that is going through an emotional breakup, you probably don't have therapist level training to ask them prying questions. When in doubt, ask them if they feel triggered, remind them that you mean well and that you can skip that topic completely until such a day they might be ready to talk about it. Some topics, like politics, race and religion, are incredibly sensitive to most people, so if you stumble on such a question, preface it with a reminder that they can skip any question. The most challenging questions have been marked with a "⚠" icon.

4. Be Vulnerable

You've already heard us say "ride your edge". What that means is that if there's something you're nervous about saying, then it's usually a massive flashing sign that you should say it. If you always avoid awkward conversations you'll never ask for that raise, you'll never ask out that cute person at yoga, you'll never improve or end your bad relationship, and you'll always be unhappy. These questions are good practice to become truly free in your expression. To become limitless. The people who get what they want in life are unafraid of what others will think or how they will react to their vulnerability. Daring vulnerability is not weakness. Vulnerability is one of your most potent strengths.

If you happen to be asked a question on a sensitive topic it's probably really good for you to talk about it. It's something you may have been bottling up. The very first time we tested these questions, we made one of our friends cry... and it was incredible! That only happened because she picked a challenging card, and was brave enough to talk about it. Think of crying during the game as being an overachiever. For the answerer of the question, being vulnerable means sometimes sharing ugly stories from your past, and from that something magical happens.

Most people who see you as vulnerable and open

up, will also open up. It's like magic. You cry, they might cry. You tell a story of being cheated on, they likely have a story of cheating too. You tell a dark childhood secret, there's a good chance they'll have a dark childhood secret. Depending on how well you are vibing, you might not want to tell any secrets that are too personal early on, or at very least remind the other player what is personal must stay between just you. Vulnerability leads to trust and beautiful things, but blurting out other people's secrets can break that trust. If your vulnerable stories involve other people, use the "I felt" instead of "he said" and "she said" statement.

If you've always thought it would be cool to have deep relationships, your first step is with yourself becoming vulnerable. Put it on yourself to set an example and you should quickly notice people loving you deeper, and sharing more deeply their truest feelings with you.

5. Take on a Positive Growth Mindset

Let's return to that example of being cheated on. When someone talks about that, they could easily get into a funk, but the challenge to all players is to keep their mindset positive. What does that mean? A negative mindset is *"he cheated on me, he's an asshole, and that's why I'll never love again"*. It's a downward spiral.

A neutral mindset: *"I was cheated on, and I'm sad about it, maybe I need a hug"*

The positive mindset to the same situation: *"I was cheated on, and maybe it's one of the best things that ever happened to me! It opened up new possibilities I could have never imagined. In times of great pain comes the most growth. Obviously I don't want that pain to happen to me again, but in a crazy way I'm grateful that it happened. Let me tell you what I learned..."*

Do you see the difference? In most of our questions, we have tried to put positive spins on challenging questions. *"What was the darkest moment in your life... and how did you grow from it?"*. Maybe the growth is still happening, but it's up to you to keep your mindset and the mindset of other players positive. Become excited about the limitless possibilities that can occur after a negative experience. Remind your new friend that life isn't full of problems at all. It's full of exciting challenges. Life is quite amazing.

That is mindset!

6. Balance The Heart Stuff With Playfulness

Even with your new positive mindset, you might notice occasionally that you can get overwhelmed with the "heart stuff". Ever watch a sad documentary or movie and feel hugely fatigued at the end? That's probably because the movie didn't balance out all the deep emotional stuff with some good light heartedness. Not many of us have the capacity to be serious all the time, so if you chance across three crazy heavy questions in a row, maybe you can say "*you know what, this one looks too heavy, let me find a fun one*".

7. Be Daring and Guess (when appropriate)

Have you ever met someone who only talks about themselves? They might be entertaining at first, but eventually they seem superficial and boring, because they're not showing any interest in you. People love talking about themselves, and in an ideal conversation, you both will show genuine interest in each other. However, some of us have experienced yet another fatigue when we have to answer the same questions about ourselves again and again. This is especially common if you've done a lot of job interviews or first dates. You tell the same stories again and again and you become mechanical about it.

So what's the one thing people love more than talking about themselves?

Hearing about themselves!

To most of the questions in this book, we invite you to flip the script and guess the answer for the other person. Here's an example:

"Tell me how your parents met!

That's actually a really sweet question to ask someone. Few people ask sweet questions like that, but how would you make it even more fun:

"Tell me how your parents met... no wait. I'm going to guess how your parents met, and then see how far off I was. You seem like a hippy so I bet they met at a sexy workshop."

Other playful examples might be:

- I get uncomfortable when people ask me what I do for a living, so I'm going to guess what you do based on your personality. Sound good?

- Let me be cheeky and guess what you were like as a kid.

- I have been watching the way you talk, and I have a really fun thing that I appreciate about your mannerisms. You want to guess what it is?

Now these sound like fun conversations! What makes them fun is the interactive nature, and the encouragement is to be daring and not really care if you get your guess completely wrong. It's wonderful to be wrong, and if you guess incorrectly that someone works in retail, they are probably going to smile and be curious *"oh wow, what made you say that"*. Keep that in your back pocket. Anytime you're asked a question that seems a bit boring, ask someone to guess the answer.

Susie: *"You seem pretty interesting Sam. What's something you are really good at that I don't know about?"*

Sam: *"Guess!"*

8. Know When to Take A Break

Even with your playful guessing, we all hit limits of engaged contact – especially for people not used to high levels of being present with someone – when they feel a bit fatigued. At this point you can, and should, end the game... do your own conversation, or go for a walk, part ways. Whatever. The book isn't going anywhere, but you need a little water break my friend.

9. Finish with Your Heart

Time to end the game? Notice that at the back there is a section called "Late Game Questions". These questions are reflective and you should decide yourself which ones are the sweetest to finish with. Personally we both like finishing with the *"what do we appreciate about each other"* and *"what made us feel most seen and connected"* style questions, followed by a *"can I give you a hug?"*

10. Be Limitless

The concept of "being limitless" may seem vague, so it's time to let you know why we call this limitless questions. 600 questions might seem like a lot, but you'll randomly chance on repeats, or eventually recycle the same finite questions with the same people. Most people get bored when they have to answer the same question twice. That's the wrong mindset!

You've heard of the growth mindset, now let's learn the limitless mindset. Certain questions are brilliant because you can ask them again and again. Thanks to a good friend of ours, we both fell in love with the question *"two highs and one low of the day"*. What's amazing about *"two highs, one low"* is that you can ask it to your friends or children every dinner time, and the answer will be different. But what about the question *"two highs and one low of your life"?* The low point of someone's life is not likely to change before the next time you ask.

The limitless mindset is one where the question asker and answer tap into their intelligence and do one of the following:

- **Dig deeper**
  - *"You already know I had a tough upbringing, but I'm going to dig deeper into how it affected me, how I got stronger"*
- **Modify the answer**
  - *"You already know what I answered last time, so let me pick another example."*
- **Modify the question**
  - *"Instead of high points, I'm going to ask you for two sexy high points"*

There's always more layers to a question waiting for limitless minds to discover, but to help make it easy, notice there's a section in this book of questions called "**Wildcard**". One example is:

"What are your thoughts about _____ ?
(suggest: yoga/spandex-pants/open-dating)"

Notice that any of the three suggestions work here. *"What are your thoughts about yoga"* is fun, because even if you don't do yoga, you might have a funny opinion about moms in yoga pants.

But what about the suggestions not written? We only fit three suggestions, but there are thousands of other possibilities: *"air shows"*, *"barbies"*, *"cheese"*, *"dogs"*, *"escape rooms"*, *"fudge"*, *"gelato"*, *"high ropes"*, *"illusionists"*, *"jealousy"*, *"karate"*, *"laundry"*, *"mullets"*, *"neon"*, *"opiates"*, *"politics"*, *"quilts"*, *"respect"*, *"star wars"*, *"tanks"*, *"ukuleles"*, *"voluptuousness"*, *"Weinstein"*, *"xenophobia"*, *"yesterday"*, *"zebras"*. Zebras are jerks obviously, and yes, these examples include A-Z, and there are thousands more. Every movie ever made, every topic, every war and event in history. How often does someone ask for your opinion of something?

We hope you're now getting it. Throughout this book we've underlined words that we challenge you to change, and a page at the end where you can write your own award-winning questions.

But being limitless isn't just about your creativity to ask infinite questions. It's about being infinite in your capacity to learn about other people, to listen, to care, to connect. Limitless is the state of mind you'll want to adopt. Limitless means limitless in your capacity to be vulnerable with people.

EARLY GAME QUESTIONS

If not already, read the "Quickstart to Play" at the beginning of this book. Players take turns asking questions and the answerer is encouraged to be vulnerable and is allowed to skip any question they deem uncomfortable or less-than-exciting to answer. Instead of launching straight into deep questions, we suggest you start with one or two questions in this section, because they can help you feel comfortable and relaxed ahead of the potentially deep questions in later sections.

Leaning in

Great to ask at the start of a game. Well not all of them, but maybe one. You can ask your partner to pick a number between one and seven and ask that question.

1 Are you nervous or excited about this question game?
2 Would you prefer to be asked easy questions or get grilled with some hard ones?
3 What style of questions, are you most hoping to get asked.. as in, family questions, silly hypotheticals, naughty questions or a total mix?
4 Are there any topics (family, religion, etc) that are off the table for you?
5 What are 5 things you notice about where you are right now?
6 What makes you uncomfortable to talk about with strangers?
7 Do you know what level of depth you might be comfortable with during this game?
8 What would help you feel more relaxed right now?

Body Talk

This is a little bit new-age, it will ask you to think about your body. Very woo woo.

1. If your body could talk, what would it say right now?
2. Would you like to take a deep breath right now? Maybe even two?
3. From 1-10, how tense are you right now, and what might make you less or more tense?
4. Is there anything you can adjust about your body or state to feel more comfortable right now?
5. Describe and feel this moment using your 5 senses: what do you see, hear, feel, smell, taste?

Meta

Questions can get meta!

1. What's a specific question you are really hoping you get asked?
2. What's something you hope I learn about you during this game?
3. What kind of intention (goal) should we set for this game?
4. Before we go further, are you afraid of deep connection and vulnerability? Why is that?
5. What's a question you might be nervous or even reluctant to answer? ⚠

GENERAL QUESTIONS

These questions are for everyone! Ask them to your parents, children, friends, strangers, co-workers or a romantic interest. Do keep in mind that in each subsection, the higher numbered questions are often more challenging, so if you are talking to a stranger you may like to start with the first few in each section. This section covers everything from hypothetical questions, to questions about family, work, life, dreams, vices and beyond.

When you see <u>underlined</u> words you are also challenged to change those words! For instance if the "favorite restaurant" is underlined, you could probably change it to "favorite theme park".

Hypotheticals

Who doesn't love a fun hypothetical?!

1. If you had a warning label on your shirt, what would it say?
2. If you could send a message to your younger self at any age, what and when would it be?
3. You are home alone and your house (with everything you own) catches fire. What do you save?
4. Invisibility, flight or super strength? What might that mean about your personality?
5. If you could design a <u>planet</u>, what would it look like, and who would you get to help you?
6. If you were an eccentric dictator of a small <u>island</u>, what crazy things might you do?
7. You are given many millions of dollars to create any <u>restaurant</u>, anywhere, unlimited creativity, and it will not fail. Describe it.
8. If you had a crystal ball that could answer only one question about <u>your future</u>, what would you ask?
9. With the choice of anyone in the world, whom would you want as a _____ ? *(suggest: dinner guest, charades partner, wing-person)*

10. What two underline animals would you like to switch the sounds they make?

11. If you could create a reality TV show, guaranteed to air, what would it be?

12. Would you rather: run as fast as a car, or fly as fast as you can walk? Why?

13. If you were CEO of any company, real or fictitious, what company would it be?

14. You have a pet cat, and it whispers a single sentence to you then never talks again. What's the creepiest thing it could say?

15. If you suddenly became indestructible and felt no pain, what are the craziest things you'd try?

16. If you could send a single text message to every person in the world, 1 sentence max, what would you send?

17. If you could live a year at any time and place in history and come safely back, when and where would you go?

18. If your life was a movie, what famous person would you want to play you? Bonus: what's the movie called?

19. What sport would you like to compete in professionally if you had the opportunity, ability and skill?

20. If your salary was doubled, what would you do with the extra income?

21. If this <u>year</u> were your last, how would you live? How would you desire to feel?

22. If you were obscenely wealthy, what would you indulge in?

23. If you could body swap with anyone for a day, who would you choose?

24. If you could switch lives with a celebrity for a week, who would it be? Why?

25. If you could body swap with any animal for a day, what animal would you pick? Why?

26. If you were to text 2 people with: I just wanted to say you are awesome and I love you! right now, who would they be? Why not do it?

27. If you could move anywhere and still have a livable wage, where would you like to move?

28. If you were stranded on a <u>desert island</u> and could only take <u>one person</u>, who would it be?

29. Would you want to live in a world where everyone's thoughts appeared as text above their head? Why?

30. If a crystal ball could answer any question about your past or human history, what would you ask?

31. If you met a clone of yourself, the same age as you, how would you get along?

32. The zombie apocalypse is coming, who are 3 people you want in your group?

33. You can have an unlimited supply of <u>one supermarket item</u> for the rest of your life, what is it?
34. If you started a <u>band</u>, who would be in it, and what name would you have?
35. If you could be with anyone tomorrow, doing anything, what would the day look like?

PG Playful

These questions are just playful, sometimes hypothetical, and often very short. These are safe for anyone.

1. If we met in kindergarten, what childish nickname would you give me?
2. If you could have a tiny pet <u>dinosaur</u>, what type, what size and what personality?
3. What's one of your real life superpowers?
4. If you had a *<u>theme song</u>*, what would it be?
5. What was the last show you binge watched? How did it make you feel?
6. Do you often remember your dreams, and what's the <u>coolest</u> dream you've ever had?
7. Tell us about a recent <u>guilty pleasure</u>, and why it brings you joy.
8. What are your thoughts about <u>yoga and the yogi culture</u>?

9. Who or what was a recent strange thing you Googled?

10. Do you ever have creative thoughts in the shower ever? What was the last one and was there any wisdom to it?

11. What was any random thought or idea you had while on the toilet?

12. What is a recent dream you remember? What do you feel it means?

13. What are your 2 biggest pet peeves and how have they surfaced recently?

14. What's the cheesiest line you've said or heard recently that made you smile?

15. How do you feel about puns and jokes? Bonus: what's a pun or joke you made or heard recently?

16. What are your comfort foods? What makes it feel like home?

17. If you were to draw me right now, on a pen and paper... would I be impressed or burst out laughing.

18. Can you do any accents or voices? Share!

19. Describe your relationship with.... chocolate.

20. What do you go crazy for?

21. Name two of your simple life pleasures that I don't know about.

22. What is one thing I don't know about you?

23. If we got together in a school science project, what <u>crazy contraption</u> would we <u>build</u> together?

24. What's the most <u>captivating or inspiring</u> thing you've recently <u>heard or read</u> about?

25. What are the last 5 emojis you used? (most phones keep a recent history, so show me!)

26. What's the naughtiest thing you've ever done which you later admitted to your parents?

27. What is the most embarrassing trashy <u>show or movie</u> you enjoyed?

28. What was the last personality test you did, and what were your results?

29. Do you believe alien life is out there? What might they think of humans?

Favorites

Playing favorites. Some people here might say "I don't do favorites", so you might instead ask them... "yes if you had to pick one right now".

1. Favorite <u>animal or spirit animal</u> and why?
2. Favorite flavor of ice cream?
3. Favorite alcoholic beverage?
4. Favorite <u>movie</u> and why?
5. Favorite sport you've ever played?
6. Favorite comedian and/or favorite comedy bit?

7. What are two of your favorite smells? Describe them.
8. Favorite birthday you ever had? Describe the day.
9. Favorite band or song and how it makes you feel.
10. Best book you've ever read?
11. What's your favorite way to exercise?
12. What's your least favorite <u>food</u>?
13. What's your least favorite domestic chore?

Life History

The puzzle of us is in our history.

1. What is one of your <u>best memories</u> in life?
2. What is one of your proudest achievements in life?
3. Best gift you've ever received?
4. Most meaningful gift you've ever given.
5. What is the greatest accomplishment of your life that you once doubted?
6. What's the most <u>unexpected thing</u> that's ever happened to you?
7. For what in your life do you feel most grateful?
8. What's the moment in life you felt most vulnerable?

9. What in life are you punctual for, and when are you late?
10. What's a question in life you really want to figure out soon?
11. What is the next big step in life you may have been putting off? And what 1-3 baby steps could you take to move towards it?
12. What's your next life goal and what excuses are slowing you down?
13. Take 2 minutes to tell your life story.
14. What do you know for sure now? What don't you know for sure now?
15. What in your life had the most profound impact that caused change?
16. The most _embarrassing_ moment in your life?
17. So tell me your life story in 5 sentences. :)
18. How do you desire to feel in life? What can you do or shift to feel that way?
19. Imagine you are 99 years old. Looking back at life, what was important?
20. After you pass, what would you want to be remembered for?
21. Name one thing you gave an honest try, and decided you never ever want to try again.
22. What's the best compliment you've ever been given in life?
23. What's a big life regret and how would you put a positive spin on it? ⚠

24. If you were to die tomorrow, what is the thing you wanted to tell someone that you most regret never saying? Why haven't you told them yet? ⚠

25. Do you have any hunches on how or when you might die? ⚠

26. What's something you did once that you are ashamed of? And how did you grow? ⚠

27. How did you recover after your lowest point in life? How did you grow? ⚠

28. If you could choose any year of your life to relive, which would you choose and why? ⚠

29. What part of your life <u>hurts</u> the most? ⚠

Childhood

Childhood nostalgia is an amazing way to open up.

1. What's your best childhood memory?

2. Describe your childhood.

3. Where were you born, and where do you wish you were born?

4. What's something you wish you had learned as a child?

5. What's an embarrassing story from your youth?

6. Tell us about your first <u>pet</u>.

7. Do you feel your childhood was happy?
8. What was your superpower when you were a child?
9. If you could change anything about the way you were raised, what would it be?
10. If you could go back in time, what is one thing you would tell your younger self?
11. Talk about your very first childhood friend in life and describe their smile.
12. Name three things you loved to do as a child. Are you doing these now?
13. What's a favorite <u>smell</u> from your childhood, and how did it make you feel?
14. What is something you had during childhood that you have lost and want back in your life?
15. What was your favorite <u>subject</u> during all of school and why?
16. Describe the best <u>teacher</u> you had in <u>school</u>.
17. What was the best <u>meal</u> you enjoyed as a kid?
18. What was your favorite TV show when you were a kid? What about it entranced you?
19. Can you remember a time as a kid that you made another kid <u>cry</u>? Tell me about it.
20. Recall one of your first memories of happiness.
21. What part of your lifestyle today might shock your childhood self the most?
22. What's one childhood dream that you've let drift away?

23. Close your eyes. Describe your childhood room to me in as much detail as you can remember.
24. What's one random thing you thought you wanted to achieve as an adult, when you were a child.

Recent History

Focus on what happened recently.

1. What does your "perfect" day look like?
2. When did you last <u>sing to yourself</u>?
3. When was the last time you sang for someone else?
4. What was the latest naughty food you ate?
5. What's something <u>inexpensive</u> you recently acquired that improved your life?
6. What's your most fun memory from this <u>calendar year</u>, and how might you beat it?
7. What is something fantastic that happened this week?
8. What's a deeper question you have pondered lately?
9. What do you like to say "no" to recently? What do you desire to enthusiastically say "yes" to?
10. What is something playful you have done recently? How can you play more in your life?

11. How have you made someone else <u>smile</u> recently? How can you?
12. When was the last time you cried from <u>laughing too hard</u>?
13. When was the last time you cried in front of someone else?
14. When was the last time you <u>surprised yourself</u>?
15. When was the last time you wrote a <u>poem</u>?
16. When's the last time you <u>yelled</u>?
17. Are you comfortable talking about your last heated argument with another human? ⚠
18. When's the last time you <u>cried</u> and why? ⚠

Current Situation

Talk about where you are in life now.

1. What are you doing that gets your creative juices flowing lately?...
2. What are you resisting in your life now? Where do you feel it in your body?
3. What would make your life better <u>tomorrow</u>?
4. What is one thing you've dreamed of doing for ages? Why not do it tomorrow?
5. Do you fantasize of being famous? Famous for what?

6. Before making a phone call, do you ever rehearse what you are going to say?
7. Share a current personal problem and, if it feels right, ask me for four words of advice.
8. What's your <u>happy place</u>?
9. What are 3 things on <u>your to do list</u> right now?
10. What's a personal goal you set for yourself recently?
11. Starting things and not finishing them. Is it an issue for you, and if so, what's something you could do to increase your follow-through in life?
12. Would you consider yourself trustworthy for <u>keeping secrets</u>?
13. What brings you joy?
14. What would you <u>change</u> about yourself now?
15. How do you hope people are perceiving you? And does it even matter?
16. What have you been doing for self care recently? What could you do that would be nourishing to yourself?
17. What are 3 things/people/opportunities you are grateful for now?
18. What are you looking forward to?
19. What thought keeps you awake at night? Will it matter in 5 years?
20. What do you need right now, but haven't asked anybody?

21. Do you think there is any reason you met me?
22. Do you play a musical instrument or have an instrument you'd love to learn?
23. Three things you can't live without. You tell me the first two, I guess the last one.
24. Describe the current chapter of your life in three adjectives.
25. So how are you, honestly?
26. Where in your life do you find the most chaos and how would you fix that? ⚠

Authenticity

Because the happiest people are the ones who are (close to) 100% authentic with themselves and others?

1. Who, in your life today, are you the most trusting and honest with?
2. Do you feel like you're living <u>authentically</u>? How would you be more authentic?
3. When are you most fully yourself, safe, trusting, and authentic? What does that feel like in your body?
4. When asked how you are, how often do you answer <u>authentically</u>?
5. What's the last thing you changed your mind about?

6. Who in your life can you be the most vulnerable with?

7. Do you feel deserving of all the nice things in your life?

8. Do you think there's a disconnect between how people see you, and how you see yourself?

9. What do you do to grow as a person?

10. Are you comfortable staring into someone's eyes for 60 seconds? Should we try?

11. If there's one person in your life you wish you had more in depth time with, who would it be?

12. Finish this statement: "My name is _____ and I stand for the possibility of _____".

13. Tell me one lesson you learned really quickly, and one lesson that took forever, or is still underway?

14. What is your calling in life?

15. How afraid are you of <u>failure</u>?

16. Is there anyone in your life you are not authentic with? How might you change that relationship? ⚠

17. How often do you lie to protect people's feelings? ⚠

18. Can you share a recent lie you felt guilty about? ⚠

19. Admit something to me that you rarely admit to anyone. ⚠

20. When did you last break a big promise? ⚠

Kindness

So beautiful it gets its own section.

1. What type of <u>compliment</u> do you most appreciate from others?
2. What do you get the most compliments about in your day-to-day life?
3. When was the last compliment you gave to a stranger?
4. Do you wish you were able to compliment and be kind more often? Explain.
5. What is the <u>kindest</u> thing a stranger has ever done for you?
6. What is a recent kind thing you did for a stranger?
7. What's a charity or volunteer event you felt strongly about?
8. Who is the kindest person you know? How do they show it?

Spirituality and Religion

Do you believe in something larger than yourself? An energy, or a god...

1. Are you religious, and how much of that is from your parents?
2. Do you follow any specific teachings or mentors? Why?

3. What's a religious or spiritual thought you've pondered lately?
4. What's something a little woo-woo you may have done recently or in the past?
5. Do you live your life by any piece of advice or motto? Explain.
6. Are you living in flow? What helps you get into flow?
7. Is there a word, phrase, mantra, prayer, or quote that would bring you some peace right now? Say it and feel some peace.
8. What does <u>enlightenment</u> mean to you?
9. What is the kindest thing you can do for yourself when you're in pain (either physical or emotional)?

Pandemic

Let's acknowledge this huge 2020 event that changed our lives forever.

1. What positive things did the pandemic bring?
2. What are 3 things you've learned about _____ during the pandemic?
   (suggest: yourself/the-world/humans)
3. What did you most miss during the first pandemic lockdown?
4. Did you lose any friendships over the pandemic?

Family

Not all families are happy families, remember that if you land on this section.

1. Who are your family members?
2. What does your relationship with your parents look like now?
3. When was your relationship with your parents the most special?
4. What do you love most about your _____?
   (suggest: mother/father/sibling/friend)
5. What do you admire most about your
   _____? (suggest: mother/father/sibling/friend)
6. How close and warm is your family? What cultivates your best moments?
7. What's the most amount of trouble you've ever been in with your parents?
8. Do you ever wish you had an extra sibling? Explain.
9. Describe your relationship with your _____.
   But only pick 5 adjectives.
   (suggest: mother/father/sibling/friend)
10. Describe your relationship with your <u>father</u>. But only use 5 words or noises.
11. Is there anything in life you are desperately trying to prove to your parents or yourself?
12. What's the last thing you <u>lied to</u> your parents about?

13. What was your most wonderful goodbye?

14. What does unconditional love look & feel like?

15. What are two things or traits about your _____
    you want to replicate in your own life?
    (suggest: mother/father/sibling/friend)

16. How often do you argue with your parents, and
    do you remember the last argument?

17. Do you have any friends or family with a
    <u>physical or intellectual disability</u>? How has that
    affected you?

18. Are your parents still in love?

19. Which family members do you wish you were
    closer to? How easy would that be to achieve?

20. Are your parents still together? Should they
    be? ⚠

21. Was there a <u>death</u> in your family or friends that
    profoundly affected you? ⚠

Parenthood

*Do you have or want kiddies!? Be warned that this
section could be challenging for some, so feel free
to skip.*

1. If you have or had children, what are the top
   virtues you'd want to instill in them.

2. If you have kids, talk about them now!

3. What are the greatest lessons you've learnt from your own children, or children you know?
4. Do you think you are, or would be an amazing parent?
5. What are your greatest fears about having or raising children?

Friends

Because people can light up when they talk about friends.

1. Talk about your <u>very best friend</u>.
2. How do you think your friends describe you?
3. What do you value most in a friendship?
4. What can your friends always count on you for?
5. What does friendship mean to you?
6. Who knows you the best out of anyone? Why?
7. Do you feel like you make friends easily? Was that always true?
8. Describe what a perfect friend would look like to you.
9. What's an experience or adventure you wanna have with your friends soon?
10. What does community mean to you and how are you building it now?
11. Which friend is your greatest <u>cheerleader</u>?

12. How have you given to others recently? How can you be even more giving and thoughtful in your life?
13. How does one earn a spot as one of your closest friends?
14. Has a friend ever betrayed your trust and how could you have handled it more gracefully? ⚠

Travel

If the world is a book then people who never travel have only read one page.

1. What's the <u>best trip</u> you've ever been on? Do you remember the sounds and smells?
2. If you could travel tomorrow without cost or responsibility, where would you go?
3. What trip or travel experience has most affected your outlook on life.
4. What is your adventure level in travel, on the scale of the all inclusive package to off the grid with only a backpack.
5. Have you ever traveled to or lived in a <u>developing country</u>? How did it change you?
6. Tell me your most <u>crazy</u> travel story.
7. How much do you love <u>camping</u>?
8. Tell me about your latest or dream adventure.

Traits

What personality traits really define a person. Let's find out.

1. How would you describe yourself in <u>three words</u>?
2. What do you think is your biggest personal flaw?
3. How do you help others smile and feel joy?
4. What's one thing you love about yourself so much you'd never change it.
5. What's something strangers who meet you would never guess about you?
6. How do you think your friends describe you to strangers?
7. What do you think your most defining characteristic is?
8. What can't people count on you for?
9. In what ways are you <u>privileged</u>?
10. How good or bad are you at <u>goodbyes</u>?
11. What's the best way people can help or comfort you when you are upset?
12. Do you have trouble quieting your mind?
13. When was that last time you acted truly brave?
14. What is your most <u>antisocial tendency</u>?
15. Is there anything about me you find intimidating? ⚠

Drugs and Alcohol

This section may be challenging for some people, but for many it involves some really funny stories!

1. Have you done any <u>psychedelics</u>? If so, tell us about one of your first times.
2. Guess how many times in life I've been high on marijuana.
3. How do you feel about cannabis?
4. What are your honest feelings about cigarettes?
5. Have you ever been peer pressured into a cigarette or other substance?
6. What was your craziest alcohol or drug experience?
7. Do you have any deep fears related to <u>drugs or alcohol</u>? ⚠
8. Have you ever been addicted to any substances? How did (or might) you overcome it? ⚠
9. Do you think you drink too much? If so, what would you change about your environment to drink less? ⚠
10. Do you have any family or friends who suffer or died from alcoholism? How are you overcoming any grief? ⚠

Growth Mindset

Mindset isn't just the title of an amazing book, the word reminds us to reframe anything that makes us unhappy and put a positive spin on it. Life is not full of problems, it is full of exciting challenges.

1. How are you approaching your <u>life</u> now?
2. How does it feel to be limitless, without boundaries, infinite?
3. What question would help you <u>grow</u> right now?
4. Deep down, who are you? Why are you here?
5. What's one limiting belief you have right now and who would you be without it?
6. What lesson is life teaching you right now?
7. What rules are meant to be broken in your life now? Is there something that's best to ask forgiveness rather than permission to do?
8. Ask me something you'd be too afraid to ask normally.
9. When was the last time you really challenged yourself?
10. What's the toughest thing, physically, you've done in your life? How did you feel afterwards?
11. What was the hardest thing you've ever done in your life? How did it evolve you?
12. The most growth often happens during heartache. Talk about how that sentence landed.

Work Related

These questions are all work related, team building and mostly work appropriate.

1. If you could tell your <u>10 year old self</u> what you do for a living, how might they react?
2. Describe your dream job.
3. What's did you learned this week at work?
4. If you could quit your job, what's the first thing you'd do?
5. What is your current career path, and what do you wish you were doing?
6. What's the <u>worst</u> thing about your workday?
7. What is one work goal you recently set for yourself, and why?
8. What was the <u>worst job</u> you ever had?
9. Do you love working from home or would you rather be in the office, or some mix of the two?
10. What do you love most about the people you <u>work with</u>? Any favorites?
11. What's the hardest part of your job? How could you make it fun?
12. Have you ever been fired from a job?
13. Who's the best boss you ever had?! Why?
14. What kind of hours do you work? Should it be more or less?
15. Do you kind-of actually hate your job?

Ice Breakers

Some of these are deliberately ridiculous.

1. What's one thing you noticed about this room/place?
2. Pick one person you see, and describe something you love about their outfit
3. Who was your childhood actor or actress crush?
4. Have you ever been told you look like someone famous? Who?
5. What's the most embarrassing fashion trend you used to rock?
6. You have to sing karaoke, what song do you pick? Describe your stage presence.
7. Do you think you take too many selfies?
8. What would the title of your autobiography be?
9. What Disney character most spoke to you?
10. Are you a morning songbird, night owl or a hybrid? Why?
11. Have you ever completed anything on your bucket list?
12. What's your best <u>scar or broken limb</u> story?
13. What's your relationship with tea and coffee? How do you take it?
14. Have you ever had a fun idea for an invention?
15. What's the weirdest food you've ever eaten?

16. What's one unique or cool feature you might add to your dream house?

17. Have you ever set a custom wallpaper for your phone or computer? What was it?

18. If you had to eat one meal everyday for the rest of your life what would it be?

19. Do you have any sports you passionately play or follow?

20. What languages do you know how to speak, or wish you could speak?

21. What do my clothes tell you about me?

22. How messy is your car or (if no car) your bedroom? Describe its current state in detail.

23. What's your relationship with pet plants and pet animals?

24. Finish this sentence: I feel excited when …

25. Do you party too much, or not enough?

26. When was the last time someone surprised you?

27. Do you party too much, or not enough?

28. Who is a person who has no idea they impacted your life?

29. What amazing memories of rain do you have?

30. Have you ever met a celebrity in real life?

31. What song has the biggest history of bittersweet for you?

32. What's the most amount of trouble you've been in with the law? ⚠

DATING QUESTIONS

Be warned that these questions are not for everyone! They range from cute questions about your first kiss and dating preferences, and escalate up to saucy questions about your wildest sexual experiences and fantasies. You probably won't want to ask these questions to a work colleague or your sibling. Even among sex positive friends, some of these questions can trigger strong emotions.

If it is a lover that you are partnered with, you'll hopefully be comfortable enough to throw in your own amazing questions, like "what are 2 things I do that drive you wild, and 1 thing I do that I could substitute with something different".

Romance

These are well suited for dates as they can be flirty! Don't use these ones on your workmates.

1. If you had a <u>warning label</u> on your back for your date, what would it say?
2. Where's the <u>most exciting</u> place you've ever made out?
3. What kind of <u>kisses</u> do you love most? Detail encouraged.
4. Tell us about your first <u>kiss</u>.
5. How do you feel about facial hair?
6. What do you look for in a man/woman?
7. What is your favorite idea of you and your partner setting the mood for a night of great romance?
8. Describe the first person you've ever had a crush on when you were little?
9. What turns you on more: slow dancing, slow kissing, or a slow caress of your legs?
10. What's your honest reaction when you see people <u>kissing in public</u>?
11. What are your feelings on PDA? (public displays of affection)
12. If we were to do a weekend getaway, what would we do?

Love

These are well suited for dates as they can be flirty! Don't use these ones on your workmates.

1. What roles do <u>love and affection</u> play in your life?
2. What are your biggest love languages?
   (physical touch, words of affirmation, quality time, acts of service, gifts)
3. How many times in life have you been in <u>love</u>?
4. How would you describe love, with as few words as humanly possible? Bonus for just one word.
5. Do you fall in love easily? Explain.
6. Tell me about your first love.

Dating

These are well suited for dates as they can be flirty! Don't use these ones on your workmates.

1. What's something <u>embarrassing</u> that happened on a date?
2. What's something not on your dating profile that I should know about?
3. Describe the best date you've ever been on.
4. Love or lust?

5. What are some great things for you and your match to have in common?

6. Have you ever played <u>matchmaker</u>? How did that go?

7. What's the most embarrassed you've ever been in your dating history?

8. How often do you take photos of yourself hoping for a better online dating pic?

9. Have any of your former lovers had interesting piercings? How was that?!

10. If you wrote a book about your dating history, what title would you give the book?

11. Describe your relationship with physical contact like <u>hugs</u>.

12. What's your <u>biggest complaint</u> about dating? How might you flip the script?

13. Be honest, are you great at handling rejection in dating? How could you get better?

14. What has been your <u>biggest revelation</u> in your dating life?

15. What are two first date experiences your friends have had that you wish you had?

16. Is there a person in your life you really wish you could set up with their <u>dream partner</u>?

17. What was your worst date? What silver lining?

18. What's been your <u>biggest struggle</u> in dating?

19. What's been your <u>biggest regret</u> in dating? What did you learn? ⚠

20. Wow, you just picked THAT QUESTION. Do you see any sexy possibilities with me, or a great friendship where I'm your wingman/wingwoman? (or your can skip if uncomfortable) ⚠

Sexuality

Let's talk about sexuality.

1. How much do you associate with your feminine side and masculine side?
2. Have you ever questioned your sexuality?
3. What is your relationship and feeling towards the LGBT community?
4. Can you expand every word of LGBTQIA as quickly as possible?
5. Share a story about any friend you have had who has changed gender or came out as gay.
6. What are your thoughts on non-monogamy?
7. Many scientists describe sexuality as a fluid spectrum from heterosexual to homosexual and beyond. Where do you think you fall? ⚠
8. Have you ever kissed someone of the same sex... or wondered what it would be like? ⚠

Flirty

These are well suited for dates as they can be flirty! Don't use these ones on your workmates.

1. How do you feel about people who own massage tables?
2. If your orgasm was a fruit, what type of fruit would it be?
3. Love or lust?
4. What's the naughtiest picture you've ever sent anyone?
5. Why are you single? (if not single: skip! duh)
6. Have you ever tried the famous "36 questions to fall in love" published in the New York Times?
7. Have you ever given nicknames for your dates among friends? If so, give two examples and explain.
8. Do you have a <u>sexy face</u> you give to get a guy or girl's attention? Show it!
9. What's something <u>inherently non-sexual</u> that someone can do that turns you on?
10. If you were to give me a <u>sexy nickname</u>, what would it be?
11. What's the most embarrassing pickup line you've ever heard or tried?
12. What do you go wild for?

13. What kind of <u>tattoos</u> might you find sexy and what isn't sexy?
14. Have you ever been described as a flirt? Why?
15. Do you have a <u>celebrity crush</u>? Do you think I could guess who?
16. When was your last full body massage?
17. Is it okay to fake <u>an orgasm</u>? If so, when?
18. Who is the most recent person you have a crush on?
19. What are your top red flags in dating? What are your green flags?
20. Tell me about your last orgasm.
21. What's your favorite <u>alcoholic drink</u>? What do you think that means about you in bed?
22. You're on a lovely date, you haven't kissed yet, but you see a couple having sex on the beach. How do you react?
23. What's the sexiest way someone could ask for a first kiss? (<u>www.consenttokiss.com</u>)
24. Describe your perfect massage from a lover.
25. If you and I dated, and you wanted to give me a nickname, what nickname would you give?
26. How often is it important to set the mood before getting naughty?
27. Describe a moment when you _____ .
    (suggest: gave-flowers/got-lucky/orgasmed-unexpectedly/broke-the-rules/got-slapped)

Sex Basics

Let's talk about sex, baby.

1. Describe yourself <u>in bed</u>, in three words.
2. When did you first <u>have sex</u> and how was your experience?
3. What is your favorite sexual position, and why?
4. How slowly do you like your partner to start sex and how do you like things progressing?
5. What's the <u>naughtiest word</u> you like being called in bed?
6. What do you love most about your partner in bed? If single, make up a partner.
7. What is the greatest thing about sex?
8. How much talk and playfulness (eg: tickling etc) should there be during sex?
9. What is the best way your partner can make you feel <u>special after sex</u>?
10. What's a fun thing more couples should do during sex?
11. Do you feel a little disappointed if your partner orgasms and not you?! How might they help?
12. What position do you find it easiest to orgasm in and/or get the most satisfaction?
13. How often do you like to take charge / instigate sex?

Naughty Sex

Oh now we are talking!

1. If you could have sex just once in any exotic location on earth, with any <u>celebrity</u> (or celebrities) where and who would it be?!
2. How often do you like to <u>pleasure yourself</u>?
3. Do you like or want to be <u>spanked</u>?
4. What would you say to the idea of your partner sending you a naughty <u>picture</u>?
5. Do you or have you ever owned any sex toys or sex games?
6. Have you ever visited a <u>sex store</u>?!
7. How comfortable do you feel telling your partner about sexual experiences you've tried in the past (before meeting you)?
8. How comfortable, jealous and/or turned on do you feel hearing your partner talk about their past sexual experiences?
9. What's a favorite way to undress your partner?
10. When was the last time you had sex while still wearing clothes?
11. Where on your body do you most love to be <u>nibbled</u>?
12. What's the most <u>unexpected thing</u> someone's done to you during sex?

13. Rate your sexual adventurousness from 0 (conservative) to 10 (whips, chains and wild AF).

14. What's the best thing your lover can do with your <u>nipples</u>? In detail.

15. Have you ever had sex outdoors and where would you most like to try next?!

16. Have you ever had sex in water and did you enjoy it?

17. Do you have any fantasies or experiences you don't usually share with other people?

18. Do you think it might be fun to be tied up or <u>blindfolded</u>?

19. What is the costume / role play you'd most want to see your partner show up as!

20. If asked to write a sex story (or maybe you have) what fantasy of yours would you write about?

21. Have you ever tried or want to try tantra or mindful sex?

22. Would you like your partner to tie you down and do naughty things to you? What things?

23. What's the sexiest sound in the universe?

24. Have you ever had sex on a _____ ?
(suggest: couch/bean-bag/shower/office-chair/
kitchen-bench/dining-table/stairs/pool-table/etc)

Body Image

Because we all have body issues. Even models.

1. What's your <u>favorite</u> part of your body?
2. Is there anything you wish you could change about your body?
3. What was the last thing you said to yourself in the mirror?
4. Describe how you usually dress (describe what you usually wear in <u>public</u>).
5. What outfit do you own, or once owned, made you feel the sexiest?
6. When are you most self-conscious about your body?
7. What moment in life did you feel the most beautiful?
8. Describe and show us the face and pose you usually make in photos?
9. What's your favorite body part..... on your lover?   (if single: skip or imagine your dream lover)
10. What's your level of comfort with nudity in front of a new lover? How about strangers on a beach?
11. Do you think you are attractive? ⚠

Safe Sex

These are some serious questions around sex and boundaries.

1. How good are you at expressing your sexual boundaries and consent?
2. How good are you at sexual consent? How could you get even better?
3. What did your last safe sex conversation look like (honestly) and how much better should it have been?
4. Guys who give warning that they want to kiss you. Sexy or shy?   (if shy: we challenge you to visit www.consenttokiss.com)
5. From who, if anyone, did you receive a good sexual education?
   Finish the sentence: Some of my boundaries around intimacy include: ...
6. What's the most irresponsible sex you've ever had in relation to poor communication around safe sex? ⚠
7. Would you be willing to simulate a real safe sex talk right now? ⚠
8. When were you last tested for STDs? ⚠
9. Have you ever had a pregnancy scare? ⚠

Relationship

Because intimacy isn't truly great unless your relationship is great.

1. Describe your <u>ideal romantic</u> relationship.
2. What couple do you know, best represent the type of relationship that you yearn for?
3. What's the most lovely thing you learned about yourself because of a relationship?
4. How would you measure the success of a relationship?
5. What unhealthy patterns in dating and/or relationships are you scared to repeat? How could you work to prevent this?
6. What does it feel like to love fully? What does it feel like to allow yourself to be loved fully?
7. If all of your exes met at a party, what's one complaint they might all share?
8. How do you typically handle <u>conflict</u> in a relationship? How would you like to improve?
9. What is your <u>greatest fear</u> in a relationship?
10. What did you appreciate most in a past relationship that you would like to recreate?
11. When was the last time you texted or called up an ex while drunk? What did you say?
12. Have you ever checked an ex's phone for evidence of misplay. Do you think I have? ⚠

Turn Ons

Because we all have stuff that turns us on!

1. What turns you on?
2. What's a sexy question you would love to answer, that I have never asked?
3. What's your favorite form of <u>foreplay</u>?
4. What is an unexpected way to turn you on <u>during sex</u>?
5. What <u>smells</u> turn you on?
6. How sexy do you find <u>high heels</u>?
7. Name a <u>sound or words</u> that drive you wild.
8. At what point in this game have you felt turned on? (if it's early: skip this question)
9. What puts you in the mood for a hot night of sex?

And that's the end of the dating section! Did you want spicier? We wanted this book to be *relatively* parent friendly, but you can find much spicier questions on our online game if you play in spicy mode!

INTERACTIVE

This section of questions is interactive because it might involve you doing an action, like sending a sweet text to someone you know, swapping seats, shaking your arms. It also, importantly, includes a "Wildcard" section where the asker is given most of the question but has to fill in the blank. Don't worry, suggestions are provided, but you get points for creativity and the best of players will realize that you can actually turn almost any question in this game into a wildcard by changing one or two words. "What's your favorite color and why?"... could become a favorite meal, celebrity, novel, dream, sexual fantasy or more. Shake it off!

Interactive

*These are questions that might involve you to
actually act something out, or sing or maybe*
even dance a little.*

1. Text one person right now: Whenever you
    cross my mind you make me smile.
2. What's the most recent song lyric you sang out
    loud? Can you sing or whistle it right now?
3. What's your favorite <u>silly dance move</u> to do,
    and will you show me?
4. Describe your relationship with your best friend
    in an accent. We both have to agree on what
    accent you pick.
5. Do you have a silly or scary face you like to
    make to amuse children? Show us, or recall
    the last time you took joy in a silly face.
6. Describe a favorite meal by imagining it on
    your tongue, in such a way that I can imagine
    I'm there sharing the same meal.
7. If you had to make a loud <u>animal noise</u> right
    now, what noise would you make?
8. If we change seats right now, do you think
    you'll miss your old seat? Let's try.
9. What's your favorite joke you like to tell people,
    or the last joke that made you laugh?
10. Should shake our arms or booty for a bit?

11. What are you like when drunk? Three choices: (1) you tell me, (2) I guess, (3) I imitate my idea of you drunk.
12. Pull my finger and I'll make an unexpected noise. Not that noise, I promise. Probably.
13. True eye gazing is in total silence, looking directly into one eye only and done properly it can be powerful. Would you like to try?
14. If I was to look at the last 10 photos you took, what might I see? Can we try it?
15. Would you like to stare at, and describe my eyes in detail.
16. Should we hold hands and take deep breaths together? How many breaths?

Guess About Me

Sometimes it's really fun to just guess something about a person, if you haven't already flipped any question back with Guess, this section will force your hand.

1. Guess how many shoes I own, and what purposes they cover?
2. Guess what I love most about myself.
3. Guess a song makes me light up and dance.
4. Guess what I <u>crave</u> more of in my life.
5. Do you think I've met my calling?

6. Based on what you know about me, what Netflix series would you recommend to me?

7. Describe my <u>perfect lover</u>, based on what you think I want and need most.

8. What country do you think I most want to visit, and why?

9. Do you think I pride myself on creativity or logic and why?

10. Do you think that I dance often, and what's my go-to style on the dance floor?

11. Do you think I can guess your favorite movie?

12. Who do you think my celebrity crush is?

13. If I were to get a tattoo one day, what do you think I'd pick?

14. If I whispered to you hey, I actually have a superpower, what do you think it would be?

15. How do you imagine I acted out as a child?

16. How outgoing and popular do you think I was in school?

17. What's the first thing you noticed about me?

18. What's the most uniting thing we have in common?

19. What's a silly expression or phrase you could imagine me saying?

20. What's something in life you think I'm probably acing?

21. What would be a perfect birthday gift for me?

22. What do you think keeps me awake at night?

23. Do you think I've ever told someone I love them, but not meant it?
24. What do you think I'll be like when I'm older?
25. What's a thing in life you think I might <u>fail</u> at?
26. What's something <u>peculiar</u> you can imagine me doing in spare time when nobody is watching?
27. What kind of <u>instagram</u> profile do you think I'm rocking?
28. What do you think the inside of my <u>fridge</u> looks like?
29. What do you think is my relationship with <u>ice-cream</u>?
30. What do you think I'm most likely to blow my cash on?
31. What do you <u>admire</u> about me?
32. What do you think makes me <u>jealous</u>?
33. What do you think my <u>biggest weakness</u> is?
34. What about me makes the least sense?
35. What about me surprises you the most?
36. What was your first impression of me when I first said hello?
37. What do you think I was good and bad at during school?
38. What are your parents' names? Based on just their names I'm going to guess what they are like and how they met.

39. Look closely and make any observation about my face.
40. Make any assumption about me.
41. Identify one thing about me you find odd or intriguing.
42. Close your eyes right now (pause) and describe what I'm wearing and the color of my hair and eyes. It's harder than you think.
43. What would you love me to say to you right now?
44. If we took a selfie together with silly faces, what face would you make?
45. If today was my birthday, and you had only 10 minutes to buy me a present, what might you get?
46. Is there anyone else in your life I remind you of?
47. Is there anything intimidating about me to you or to others?
48. Based on my appearance alone, what would you assume about my personality and level of kindness?
49. Can you translate my body language into a sentence right now?
50. What might change between us, to make you feel closer to me?

Wildcard

Fill in the blank as you ask the question. Bonus if you go beyond the suggestions.

1. _____ ?

2. When were you last _____ ?
   (suggest: afraid/giggly/horny)

3. Tell me the story behind your
   _____ ? (suggest:
   necklace/hair/sweetness)

4. I have a question about your hobbies!
   _____ ? (suggest: want/biggest/coolest)

5. I have a question about your family!
   _____ ? (suggest: favorite-memory/best-hugger)

6. List 3 things you think you have in common
   with _____ ? (suggest:
   me/your-mom/Obama/sherbet)

7. In a sexy way... describe your relationship with
   _____ ? (suggest: pizza/yoga/sleep)

8. What puts you in the mood for _____ ?
   (suggest: going-to-bed/hot-sex/work)

9. Have you ever had a perfect _____ ?
   (suggest: day/poop/gelato)

10. Have you ever experienced a _____ ?
    (suggest: mai-tai/steakhouse/surf-lesson)

11. What was your last _____ on the
    Internet?
    (suggest: search/amazon-purchase/song)

12. What's your relationship with _____ ?
    (suggest: sleeping-in/cookies/music/technology)
13. _____. Thoughts?
    (suggest: cross-fit/facial hair/Japanese porn)
14. What would support you to feel more
    _____ right now?
    (suggest: free/joyful/comfortable/connected)
15. What are your thoughts about _____ ?
    (suggest: yoga/bike-pants/open-dating)
16. Have you ever tried _____ ?
    (suggest: yoga/yodeling/skydiving/tango)
17. Tell me a favorite _____ .
    (suggest: musical instrument/animal/flower/place)
18. What was the most _____
    (intriguing/nourishing/hopeful/strange) part of
    your _____ (day/week)?
19. What _____ you recently?
    (inspires/surprises/relaxes/motivates/scares)
20. What is your relationship to _____
    recently? Is there a practical step you could
    take to improve this relationship? (suggest:
    technology/time/your-mind/your-body/your-family)
21. Deep down, what are you afraid of in
    _____ ?
    (a-relationship/starting-something-new)
22. What are 3 things you discovered about
    yourself during _____
    (the-pandemic/your-childhood/this-past-year/high-
    school)

23. What could you shift to make your life better
    _____ ? (tomorrow/today/right-now/next-year)
24. What is a _____ from childhood? Describe
    it and how it makes you feel.
    (suggest: smell/taste/memory)
25. What was the last thing you _____ ?
    (suggest: threw-out/crossed-off-a-list/clapped-for)
26. When was a memorable time someone
    _____ ? (suggest: kicked-you/farted/helped-
    you/loved-you/doubted-you)
27. Rate your _____ between 0 and 10.
    (suggest: driving-skills/playfulness/banter/animal-
    noises/ping-pong-skills)
28. What's your favorite form of _____ ?
    (suggest: art/music/transport/fun)
29. Where were you the last time _____ ?
    (suggest: you-cried/you-won-something/you-lost-
    something)
30. What's a person's name you think is _____ ?
    (suggest: silly/pretentious/badass/awkward)
31. Tell me any memory you have involving a
    _____ . (suggest: park-bench/snake/waterbed/
    frog/snake/surfer/christmas-tree)
32. What does the word _____ mean to
    you? (suggest: love/loyalty/connection/racism/
    god/hustle/capitalism/trust/diet)
33. Explain your feelings about _____ ?
    (suggest: the-police/guinea-pigs/matt-damon)

LATE GAME QUESTIONS

All good things come to an end, and we recommend you finish the game with at least one or two questions in this section. These questions focus on reflection and strongly encourage you to end with a hug or telling the other player what you appreciate most about them.

At this stage you might not even be random, but realize that there's a question you really want to ask, such as "was there any point at this game you felt moved".

Leaning Out

Great to ask at the end of a game. A focus on reflection.

1. When in this game or today did you feel the most connected?
2. Was there a point in this game where you felt <u>embarrassed</u>?
3. Is there anything about yourself that you have <u>learned</u> by talking to me?
4. Is there any aspect of your life you think I could help inspire you?
5. What answer that I gave seemed the most <u>vulnerable</u>?
6. What are 3 things you <u>appreciate</u> about me?
7. Was there any question or topic you are disappointed that we missed?
8. What's something you have taken from this experience?
9. **If this is a date**: were there any moments in the game you felt turned on?
10. **If this is a date**: was there any point in the game you wanted to kiss me?

Moving On

What happens now?

1. Would you like to share a hug?
2. What do you think would be a perfect way to end this game?
3. What happens next?

Making Your Own Questions

Hopefully you're already feeling inspired by this book! We feel like we've given you enough examples so you can start to extrapolate your own question. Do you disagree? Well fuck you! Just kidding. As part of the growth mindset you might easily come across some questions you dislike and trigger you, but the fun thing you can do is make this book your own. Highlight your favorite questions, cross out the ones that don't serve you, and extrapolate some of your own questions below:

_____

_____

_____

_____

_____

_____

Taking it to the Next Level

If you have just finished reading all 600 questions, we're hoping you're feeling inspired to try some! No mere mortal could possibly memorize all these questions, but we hope you have identified one or two questions that either deeply resonate with you or made you giggle, and that you're excited to try out on friends, coworkers or even on dates. Job interviewers will tell you that it's not about knowing a thousand different questions, but identifying a few really amazing questions and perfecting them through practice.

At the start of the book you learned 10 amazing principles, including (1) active listening, (2) escalate vulnerability, (3) being sensitive to triggers, (3) being vulnerable, (4) taking on a positive growth mindset, (5) balancing deep stuff with playfulness, (6) guessing the answer, (8) taking breaks, (9) finishing with the heart, and (10) being limitless.

Now we have five more principles to take your question-based conversation to the next level:

1. **Be Versatile**

2. **Be Open (zero judgment)**

3. **Be Passionate**

4. **Be Bold**

5. **Follow Up and Keep Integrity**

1. Be Versatile

Do you think the Dalai Lama walks away from any conversation to tell his friends *"Jesus, that was boring as s**t"*? Heck no! The Dalai lama is enlightened enough to realize that every person on earth has a unique and beautiful story. A treasure chest of beautiful unique moments. The challenge we give to you is to open that chest, or at very least, have fun trying.

Let us tell a small story about one of our dearest friends, and let's call her Tina. During the late pandemic we encouraged Tina to try online dating, and she lit up when she started meeting some very accomplished and interesting eligible men. Five in a row in fact!

We told her she had statistically hit a golden run. Even with the best filtering on online dating it's normal to meet "duds" - people who might seem uncomfortable, boring or a completely different wavelength – and we gave our own unique advice on how she might handle such a date. Sure enough, date number six she finally got her complete online dating experience whereby she met a dud. It's not that he wasn't a great guy, he just wasn't a guy for her. She didn't shut him down immediately though, she said she remembered our advice and flipped it around into something positive. She found the humor and even though it wasn't a spectacular date, it had some lovely memorable moments of insight.

Often in life you're going to have to talk to people you don't vibe with and you maybe even find unpleasant. That's okay! Maybe it's the aging relative that rambles, a friend's kid with horrible ADHD, a loud relative from Texas with outrageous political opinions, a monosyllabic teenager who only answers "*I dunno*", a business accountant that only seems to talk about frisbee golf. You can't always hang with fun and good looking party animals your age, and honestly, if you do then it's probably quite bad for you. A well-rounded person can talk effectively with anyone, they can adapt, they can listen, and they gain their wisdom by talking and listening to a wide array of people, including those with different life outlooks.

So next time you meet a seemingly shallow girl from LA who gossips incessantly, or that douche white trust-fund muscles-shirt guy with hair gel boasting about his new car, get curious about an undiscovered later that possibly no other human on earth has seen. People who act as if their poop doesn't smell are often the ones with the most insecurity and you can humanize almost anyone when you open them up. People are all beautiful puzzles and if you're having a boring time with someone, you can tell yourself it's their fault for being boring.... or you can admit that it takes two people to tango, and you simply haven't found the right question to spark their passion. Maybe what they need is to see you light up talking about a story, *"let me tell you a story about the best present I was ever gifted in life"*, and that will inspire them. Maybe you need the right observation, *"I've noticed that when you talk you brush your hair, and it's really fun to watch. It makes me imagine you as a little girl with pigtails and it makes me wonder what dreams you had when you were a kid. You're wildest dream in life"*.

We like to imagine ourselves as the heroes of our narrative, but what if we watched a movie about their life story. If someone seems terrible, imagine that they've had a hard life, and imagine they are the hero of the movie, not us. We might just be a cameo appearance, but we should be a positive appearance. You can generate interest and self amusement with anyone you talk to, and one of life's challenges is to be able to bring joy to any person, not just the people we consider "fun". If you can relate and connect with the full spectrum of humanity, from rich to homeless, from wild to conservative, from old to young, then everyone around you will light up with excitement.

2. Be Open (zero judgment)

Let's return to the example of political differences. Can someone liberal and conservative be friends? One hundred percent they can! There's every chance they are both insanely friendly and wonderful people.

What about deeper moral differences though. We also have vastly different morals and we're quick to judge people who go against our own values. Maybe it's someone who lies, someone who smokes, someone who cheats, someone addicted to hard drugs, someone who shoots animals, someone who worships a god, someone who doesn't worship a god, someone who supports a narcissistic, someone who lives in a van, someone who has done questionable things to a person or animal, someone who doesn't support gay marriage, someone who committed a serious crime. We're all human and if born into their family we'd likely be in their shoes. The world can always use more compassion.

Early in the book we gave an example of being cheated on, but actually one of our most memorable moments in the game has been meeting people who were the "cheaters". Just for the balls to admit this, we had respect, and quickly we realized that cheating is rarely a black and white. To paint someone as a villain without understanding their side of the story is to be judgmental. Often the most incredible people in our society have, in their past, deep scars and memories of committing adultery or crime. Or maybe their point of view on these events is just very different from our own, and we'd be very narrow minded to not hear them out. Once upon a time human sacrifice and slavery were perfectly acceptable, and decades from who know what behaviors we have now (eating meat for instance) we'll consider with the same contempt. Not everyone has the same cultural and moral background as we do, and to become a wiser, more balanced person is to hear all about these other cultures and points of view.

There are some arguments that might feel to us very "flat earth" naive, but you may be surprised that someone that believes cheating is not wrong, or that gay marriage is wrong, or that a conservative government is better than a liberal one... you may be very surprised to hear arguments that you've never considered before. Probably you're not about to change your mind on these issues, but it can help humanize someone who you might otherwise consider as awful in any way. The Dalai Lama would not make this mistake of not listening. Why would you? We are just human, and to listen without judgment is a beautiful gift that helps inspire better acceptance for everyone.

When someone gives you an answer that makes you question their character, check in with your own judgment, and listen with an open mind, and compassion.

3. Be Passionate

We've all met a person who just never seems to light up. We consider them boring. *"What's your favorite movie of all time and why?"*

"I dunno, I don't really like movies. I think they are lame."

Wow, thanks for killing the conversation sad sack! That answer is the opposite of playful. Here's a playful answer:

"You know, I don't watch movies often, but sometimes I like to imagine myself filming my own movie. Maybe it would be about hamsters with guns."

If you've ever gone straight from a country like the United States to almost anywhere in Europe you'll understand what passion looks like. The US has a history of high economic opportunity where putting on a facade of success and indifference is almost considered cool. Ask an American about their favorite art form or croissant and they might give a pretty flat answer.

"I guess a croissant is okay." (yawn)

Now ask a backpacker from Italy about their opinions on movies, or art, or croissant. They light up!

"I live for food! My favorite pastry shop in Paris serves a croissant that is like the Rembrandt of desserts. I almost orgasm each time I take a bite."

There are people in this world, who can get you excited. Even when they don't know the answer, they light up at the chance for self expression, or curiously to learn. These people make conversation easy. So maybe you don't naturally move your hands when you talk, but with a little practice you can learn to step up your level of animation and get people excited.

Comedy improv isn't for everyone, but they do have an amazing principle called "Yes, And". What it means, in a nutshell, is that whenever one of your partners in the comedy skit gives you a premise, you never reject it – you add to it. For instance if your partner says "Derrick, *we were told you like space*", you don't shut them down with a "*not really*", you say "*Oh my gosh, I love space so much, did you know I'm three weeks away from becoming an astronaut*". "*But Derrick you are only five*". "*I know I'm only five, but I'm pretty smart for five*".

The "Yes, And" principle can be applied throughout life as your friend says. After this game we should totally get dessert. "*Oh hell yes, we can go to the corner store to buy cookies and then dip them into ice cream*". The opposite of "Yes, And" is to say "*your idea is stupid*". These people might consider themselves realists, but they are killers of creativity, because the great doers of the world surround themselves with people who can help take the excitement of an idea and turn it into something completely different, and almost always one order or magnitude better than the original idea. Passion is necessary to manifest dreams. Passion is what excites people to turn an ordinary conversation into an unforgettable interaction.

Don't pretend you are too cool for school and give short answers or make your partner feel like an idiot. Think of yourselves as two excited kids on the school ground eager to get out and play.

4. Be Bold

Being bold is something that comes with confidence and experience, and it could mean different things to different people. Maybe you are playing this game with someone that (perhaps unwittingly) said something that profoundly upset you a month, a year or a decade ago. Get that off your chest! There is always the easy answer and then there is the vulnerable answer – the one that might improve your relationship with someone. If this is a date then "being bold" may mean asking someone out, or respectfully letting them know that you want to kiss them. Hopefully the act of asking will bring you happiness, and you'll still be proud for being bold, even if they say no. Sometimes the best way to say something really bold, is to preface it with the acknowledgment of bravery.... "*This will sound really bold, but I do think I deserve a raise*". Maybe it means telling someone about a deep sexual fantasy. Being bold might even just be saying: "*I know this isn't the current question, but I really want to ask this one to you, because it could be really deep*".

Find out what being bold in this game means to you.

5. Follow Up and Keep Integrity

Certain people and certain cultures still consider their word as their bond. If they say "*we should meet again soon*", they will. Imagine that. "*I'll text you tomorrow*". They do. Imagine that. "*I promise to keep this secret*". Throughout much of the US a "*let's catch up soon*" is typically interpreted as a "*I'm busy, and I have good intention, but that's not happening*".

The silver lining of a flaky society is that it becomes pretty easy to stand out from the crowd. Just by doing what you say you will do, can often make you seem exceptional. Maybe after your game, make a note to text the other person or people that you had an amazing time, or that a particular answer they gave really made you laugh or think deeply. This is particularly useful if you've played with someone that admits they never open up to anyone. Suddenly they might feel extra vulnerable the next day for leaving their comfort zone, and this kind of message will reinforce to them that there are caring people in the world and they should consider sharing more of themselves. That their vulnerability meant something to you beyond the few minutes that you played the game.

Keeping integrity is mostly just a reminder to keep your deepest conversations private. Maybe you're an open book kind of person, able to tell anyone your past, but the person you're talking to might be incredibly sensitive about sharing their past. That trust is sacred and it may be impossible to earn that trust in a few minutes of playing a game.

Fortunately, people are, for the most part, abiding by the consistency principle. If you tell people you have high integrity, then that will become part of your identity, and soon enough it will become true.

A Thank You From the Authors

Thank you so much for buying our book! If you are feeling inspired, what helps us the most is reviews, so please type "Limitless Questions" into Amazon and leave us a review! You can also access way more questions and more limitless questions products via the website:

www.limitlessquestions.com

As you use this book, we hope you will find yourself becoming a master of conversation. Armed with some creative juices, incredible questions and active listening skills, you might find yourself connecting deeply with people you never connected with before. We hope you enjoy the limitless possibility that lay ahead of you each time you ask someone limitless questions.

Sincerely,

Ann and Andrew

About the Authors

Andrew Noske, PhD

Andrew is a neuroscience postdoc who got his PhD in Australia studying diabetes. He left Australia to try and make an impact in the United States, and took a left turn into software engineering. He currently works as a Google Maps engineer, but his biggest passions are writing books and dancing. His first book, Ice Cream = Sex, is a fun question for first dates or playful friends.

Follow Andrew via:
www.andrewnoske.com

Ann Swanson, MS

Ann is a certified yoga therapist, speaker, and author of Science of Yoga which has been translated to 15 languages. With a Master of Science Ann is part heart-based healer and part science nerd. Ann supports people in being healthier and more joyful. She does this by making yoga and wellness non-intimidating and accessible, especially those who feel like they can't do yoga.

Follow Ann via:
www.annswansonwellness.com